A Voice in the Wind

Leeza Wilson

A Voice in the Wind © 2018 by Leeza Wilson

All rights reserved. No part of this book may be used or reproduced or transmitted in any form or by any means, electronic or mechanical, including photocopying, recording, or by any information storage and retrieval system, without written permission by the author except in the case of brief quotations embodied in critical articles or reviews.

Printed in the United States of America.
Published by Tsarina Press

ISBN: 978-1-948429-14-6

Dedication

This book is dedicated to my best friend, Christi Harris. You are more than a friend. You are my sister. We weathered so much together growing up, and I'm sure my life would not be the same had you not been in it. Though time and distance has kept us physically apart, our lives will forever be joined through sisterly love.

Table of Contents

Wicked	1
My Voice	2
Reality of Evil	3
Rescue Me	3
Recluse	4
So Lonely	5
Invisible	6
The Shape of Us	7
If Only	7
JP	8
Broken	9
Lonely	9
I Suffer Alone	10
Hanging By a Thread	10
The Pen Went Dry	11
The Attacker	12
Gone Too Soon	14
Shots Fired	16
1980 Something	17
Spinning My Wheels	18
Lost or Abandoned	19
Praying for Rain	20
A Voice in the Wind	21
Depression	22

Battled Scarred	23
Stress	24
Hidden Pain	24
Feelings	25
Forever Entwined	26
I Do	27
Disappointing	28
Violated	29
Torn Apart	30
World Gone Mad	31
I Would Rather	32
How Dare You!	33
A Cat Speaks	34
To the Hidden Beast	35
Verizon	36
Psychotic Sister	37
Alzheimer's	38
How Do You See Me?	39
Cry	40
Dreams	41
Torn	42
Where's the Music	44
Poverty	45
My Mistake	46
Haiku Poems	47
Moonlit Bay	49
Butterflies	49

Flowers	50
The River's Bend	50
The Mausoleum	51
The Eiffel Tower	51
Black Cat	52
Autumn	52
Rose	53
Masterpiece	53
Birds	54
Things That Wow	54

A Voice in the Wind

Wicked

Your lips speak wicked and twisted things
Upon your innocent victims
Mayhem and madness rains
With viperous venom from your serpent's tongue
Your ears hear not the plaintive cries
Of those who suffer from your lies
For justice from you they long
But their significance your malicious mind denies
Your shriveled, black heart only pumps
The green sludge of envy
That empowers your bitterness.
All those in your path your mischievous feet tramps
Your vulture claws rip apart
All those with a clean, pure heart.

Leeza Wilson

My Voice

I have a voice.
Weak and small, though, it may be,
It is still my voice.
Angry words at you it may scream,
Or joy and exhalation it may beam.
But it is still my voice.
Words of sorrow and grief
Or brutally honest words it may stream.
Because this is my voice
And how I use it is my choice.
To you this may be an annoyance.
But that's no matter to me,
Because after all, this is *my* voice.
My words may come out forceful and strong
Or they may drag out tired and forlorn.
No matter how my words may fall
I will be heard through it all.
Because it is my voice
And away from me it will never be torn

Reality of Evil

Why does it seem that evil triumphs over good?
When the fairy tales of our childhood
Fooled us into thinking that evil is conquered by good.
With evil's beastly jaws we are killed.
It shreds our souls for its belly to fill,
Leaving our gutted remains in a dark, winter chill.

Rescue Me

God, rescue me from this hell called life
Deliver me from poverty and strife
My heart and soul bleeds
It seems there is no reprieve
Oh, please God, rescue me!

Recluse

I really have become quite a recluse,
Happily tucked away in my house.
But why you may ask.
Well, let me give you my excuse.
The world has become cold, dark, and bitter.
It is full of others' litter.
No, not their trash,
But their hopes and dreams that've been dashed.
The world gropes to get high on hash.
And all the people want is cash.
And to build a wealthy material stash.
To obtain it they care not who they bash.
In their wretched greed they thrash.
They only set themselves up for a crash.
So I will be happy recluse.
And now you know my excuse.

So Lonely

I'm so lonely I wanna die.
I matter to on one,
No one but maybe mom.
Her health is bad and her years are great.
That makes death her impending fate.
About it I can't even think.
Oh, the loneliness that'll be pushed to the brink.
I can't imagine how my heart will break.
There's already such a deep void and ache.
To matter to no one anymore
Makes life such a humdrum bore.
Life is hard when lost in the sea
Of a cold, distant humanity.
All I ever wanted was to be loved.
I wanted to be someone's turtle dove.
But no, I live in my humble home
Where I'm all alone.
A single, empty shell
Just waiting on the gates of hell.

Invisible

No one seems to notice me.
How can that be?
What is it about me
That they cannot see?
They simply glance my way
With nothing to say.
Just like they can't see me.
I feel like I don't belong in their sea.
But with them I want to be.
Don't they know the loneliness I feel?
Please, let me make one last appeal.
Can't you please make room in your sea
For just one more of humanity?
Take just one close look at me
And a beautiful, deep soul you will see.

The Shape of Us

You said we were totally square
But it seemed all we ever did was go in circles
I wore my heart on my sleeve for you
Then you turned our love into a triangle
My tear drops flooded the rectangle we called home
Now all I have left for you
Is a bright red octagon over my heart

If Only

If only the cruel hands of dawn
Wouldn't rip me from my dreams
Where peace and happiness gleams

Leeza Wilson

JP

Training to walk through the flames
Sturdy and strong, I saw you standing there
Through the course I saw your spirit
There was no doubt the connection I felt
You were my mentor and before you I knelt
But also felt the pain that stabs your heart
Like a sister, I reached out to you
But closed off you were to me
Not allowing me to see why your heart bleeds
And so it would be until our paths did part
But a sister in service to you I'll always be

Broken

The tears come nearly every day
But I hide them in shame
I'm not supposed to be weak
The reserves of my inner strength
Should never break down and leak
Always strong I must be
My cracked soul no one else must see

Lonely

This loneliness I feel is not my fault
For I am a product of the past
This modern world moves too fast
Nowhere left for me to be
But hidden in an empty, lonely vault

I Suffer Alone

I suffer alone
I suffer in silence
No one can know
How shattered I am inside
That smile on my face
Just an empty façade
To hide the cracks of my soul

Hanging by a Thread

My faith is bruised and battered
But not totally shattered
I face each day with dread
I'm hanging onto hope by a thread

The Pen Went Dry

The pen went dry
So many lines left to write,
So many tales to tell,
But the pen went dry.
No other could take its place.
No other could make its trace.
Why did the pen have to go dry?
All that's left is to stare at the page,
To daydream of what could have been
If the pen had not gone dry.
Faded out in mid-line.
The last lines faded to nothing,
Forever lost to the black hole in space.
All because the pen went dry.

Leeza Wilson

The Attacker

There they are again
Tip-tap, tip-tap...
I stop in my tracks
Over my shoulder I glance back
No one there—only the wet black top.
Was that sound just the rain?
I begin walking again.
Tip-tap, tip-tap...
An echo of my own steps?
I pick up my pace,
Tippity-tap Tippity-tap...
I slow my pace,
Tip... Tap... Tip...Tap...
They are close and heavy steps.
I can feel a presence at my back
No, it's definitely not the rain.
My heart begins to race.
I glance over my shoulder.
A shadow darts around a corner.
I search the street
For a place to retreat.
I am seized by fear.

My heart is pounding in my ears.
Are the footsteps still there?
Who could it be?
Who could be coming after me?
Maybe it is someone I know
Who just wants to say hello.
But why hide in the shadows?
A firm hand grabs my elbow.
A quick lunge forward
Brings the attacker over.
Across my shoulder he's brought low.
His face reveals he never expected the blow.

Leeza Wilson

Gone Too Soon

Here today, gone tomorrow.
Not a phrase that should relate
To the young ones of our day.

Little girl, hair in pigtails,
A hug and kiss from mom,
"See you after school, dear."
Hours later—a devastating call.
A safe haven turned into a target range.
It only took one shot for such a little doll.
It's all over.
No more hugs from mama's little baby.
She's gone too soon.
Taken by a senseless act.

Young man with dreams.
A talented musician,
An honor roll student
Soon to graduate.
Walking in the hall to class
His close friends by his side
Talking of their college plans.

Bang! Bang! The shots ring out.
Taken by surprise.
Nowhere to hide.
He lies next to his friends as he dies.
Gone too soon.
Taken by a senseless act.

When will the madness stop?
How many more young have to die?
To the hearts of the grieving
Someone must listen to.
The blood of the slain
Cries out for justice.

Only God hears their pleas for redemption.
He knows they're gone too soon.
They rest in His memory
Safe from harm and misery.

For the ones left behind.
Earthling man cannot right the wrong.
Rest your hope in God.
Trust He will make you strong.

Leeza Wilson

Shots Fired

I woke up to gun shots today.
"Stay low, child," I heard mama say.
I clasped my tiny hands and prayed.
"Lord, please watch over our souls this day."
"Mama, why's everybody gotta carry a gun?" I say.
"Child, it's just gotta be that way.
Until some politician's child dead in the street lays,
Nothing's ever gonna change."
"Don't they know how we suffer this way?"
I saw mama drop her eyes and sigh.
With a shake of her head, mama went on to say,
"They know, child. They just don't care.
It's not a politician's affair.
It's a man's right to carry they say."

1980-Something

Oh, how I wish it was 1980-something
I would be young and carefree
I would still be in my small hometown
And my dad would still be around.
My best friend would still be close
Right across the street she would be
We would be together everyday
Laughing and dancing, happily at play
But I would dream my sister away
As she was hateful and selfish
And caused everyone stress
Duran Duran and A-Ha would be on the radio
I could still rock an 80's do
And dance to Kajagoogoo
TV would still be good
With shows like
ALF, Magnum PI, and Family Ties
Families would still sit and talk
Electronics would only be a VCR and Atari
Those were the good old days
Oh, I how I wish it was 1980-something

Leeza Wilson

Spinning My Wheels

I'm spinning my wheels…
Spinning my wheels
Staring at the sun
Just spinning my wheels
Don't know where to turn
So tired of spinning my wheels
Been trying for so long
To turn things around
But keep hitting a wall
Then things come tumbling down
Right on top my head
Nothing changes for the better
Negatives just keep piling up
So I'm spinning my wheels
Looking for solutions
Only finding mountains
Of more problems
Guess I'll always be
Spinning my wheels

Lost or Abandoned

Lost or abandoned?
Either way, I'm all alone
Thrown to the wolves
To fend on my own
For sustenance daily scavenging
In search of shelter I'm floundering
For safety and companionship I'm praying
But all of it is found only in a dream
I stand alone and scared
Peering up to the heavens I scream
A miniscule speck of dust I am
Drifting aimlessly through the air
I pray for the day
When my troubles will be wiped away
And this God-forsaken life won't last another day

Leeza Wilson

Praying For Rain

A life that is drowning
Is really no life at all
But just the same
I pray for rain
To wash away my pain
To fill my soul
That's full of holes
So I can float away
And find a happy day
A better place to stay

A Voice in the Wind

I am a voice in the wind
In futility I call out
No one hears me
My cries for help
Are stolen by the breeze
My voice muffled and muted
To the unsuspecting ears
Cries for help they do not appear
To them it seems a dull tune
They do not know
With their lives they go on
Paying no attention at all
To my voice in the wind

Leeza Wilson

Depression

DEPRESSION!
A real live monster of its own breed
A monster who wallows in greed
For it cares not who you are
Your status in life means nothing to it
The black-eyed monster of depression
Swallows up the rich same as the poor
The big and strong are no safer
Than the small and weak
Gender, race, and age make no difference
Depression sees them all alike
To hold the captives strong and tight
Depression uses a special winch
It reels the sufferers under a tent,
A tent called Mental Illness
No one wants to wear that brand
A stigma of shame
Lurks with that name
Under such a tent no one wants a place
But depression does not ask
Before stealing another smiling face
Depression covers the soul in grey

Eating it away
Only an empty shell remains
Of the soul that once was
To roam free of shame
The empty soul must don a mask
To avoid the stabs of ridicule
From daggers of well-meaning souls,
One mustn't speak of the pain inside
To those who live on the outside

Battle Scarred

I would rather laugh than cry
But life has left my heart ripped wide
I struggle against this tumultuous tide
There's no way to get free from this wild ride
Battled scarred, there's nothing left to do but hide
Emotions aswirl on the roller coaster of life
Til death my time I must abide
And til then learn to take it all in stride

Stress

Stress they say is a silent killer
This I know for sure
Rarely do I go a day without stress
Every day I feel myself dying a little more
So sick and tired of being bombarded
Smothered under the quagmire of stress

Hidden Pain

It doesn't seem to me
That anyone sees
The sadness and desperation
Behind my blue eyes
I must hide it well
That's how it should be

Feelings

Pain is all I know
Sorrow engulfs me
Shame is what I hide behind
Desperation is all I feel
Longing fills my soul
Loneliness shatters my heart
Stress is tearing me apart
Fear is taking over
Death is the only relief

Leeza Wilson

Forever Entwined

I tried to abandon you
I ran away and tried
To leave you in the past
I wanted to forget you
I tried to cut you from my heart
But I couldn't remove you from my soul
You kept calling to me
Sending me reminders of you
I tried to shut them out
My efforts were in vain
A love from youth one cannot deny
The mark of our culture
Is engrained in our life
I am yours
And you are mine
Love it or hate it
We are forever entwined

I Do

Do you want to dance
like no one's watching?
I do
Do you want to sing
like no one's listening?
I do
Do you want to play
like we did as kids?
I do
Do you want to wander freely
like you own the world?
I do
Do you want to live
like there is no dying?
I do

Disappointing

I ate a disappointing breakfast
On a cold, disappointing morning
I looked out the window
At my disappointing view
With a heavy heart
And a mind full of worry
To start the day
There was no hurry
Why should there be?
Then I went to my favorite seat
I picked up a book to read
I joined the characters
In another world
Now everything's okay
And the world's a happy place to be

Violated

You break into my home
You look at and touch my things
But you steal nothing…
Nothing but my sense of security
You shred my dignity
With the fear you spread
A growing paranoia consumes me
What will you do next?
Will you break in again
To ravage my secret places?
I feel you watching…
Waiting for your next opportunity
Will your next violation
Be worse than your first?
I'm trapped under your thumb
There's nowhere for me to run
I pray for help and a way out
But there's no benefactor to save me
So on guard I will forever stand

Leeza Wilson

Torn Apart

We were best friends by chance
But we were sisters by choice
We shared everything
Between us there were no secrets
We vowed to always stay together
But family strife and time
Were our only enemies
Your parents divorced
And distance became our obstacle
Somehow through it all we managed
To hold on to what we had
Then adult life came too soon
And we went our separate ways
Eventually we found each other again
Only to discover that nothing stays the same

World Gone Mad

A new day has dawned
A new normal has evolved
A world gone mad
Where gun fire is the norm
And fear has seized us all
Who will fall next
At the hands of a madman?
In this world gone mad
Safety does not come in numbers
The crazies prey on crowds
In this world gone mad
One's not safe anywhere you go
Even in one's home
The madness continues on
Because the world has gone mad

Leeza Wilson

I Would Rather

I would rather
Hear you laugh
Than see you cry
I would rather
Feel the warmth
Of your smile
Than see the pain
Of your frown
I would rather
Lift you up
Than tear you down
I would rather
Hold you in my arms
Than not feel your warmth
I would rather
Love you forever
Than live without you

How Dare You!

How dare you judge me!
We've only just met
You know not the fight I've fought
And the battles I'm still fighting
I will not bare my soul to you
How dare you ask me to?!
If you judge me now
With what little you know,
How can I trust you
With the deepest parts of my soul?
Your piousness has left a mark
Now an iron lock safeguards my heart
The path I walk is riddled
With the decaying bones of ones like you
I leave them in the past
With not one glance back
They are not worth my time
If all they desire
Is someone to look down upon

Leeza Wilson

A Cat Speaks

Do not belittle me
Or declare me a lesser
Just because I am small
And covered in fur
Do not think I am dumb
Because I do not speak with words
For I speak in my own way
And you are not so smart
If you do not understand
Listen closely to my meows
They will tell you what I want
Watch my whiskers too
Then you will see what I'm sensing
They will even tell you
When I'm feeling extra pleased
Observe my tail
And if it's swishing quickly
You will know I'm angry
And you should beware
Even the fur on my little body
Will tell you when I'm feeling
Threatened, nervous, or scared

So as you see,
I speak quite well

To the Hidden Beast

To the beast hidden away
You may come out and play
Only when I so say
But if you misbehave
Again you will be locked away

You should not, cannot, must not
Attack the weaker lot
Imprisoned you will be until you rot
And destroying my Luna baby you will not
Absolutely No! No! No!

So stay calm and be sweet
No creatures shall you beat
Then you will not feel punishment's heat

Verizon

You lie to your customers
Luring them in with smooth talk
And false promises you never intend to fulfil
There is no recourse for your actions
You get away with all your crimes
Because you have so much money you can
You own every lawyer known to man
Your customers have no outlet
For justice and redemption
Only the President has the power
To go against your abrasive hand

Psychotic Sister

The voices no one heard but you
The ghostly people no one saw but you
The delusions you lived by
Tore us all to shreds
Mom walked on egg shells
So afraid to anger or displease you
Poor dad lost the will to live
So convinced he'd failed us all
I grew up confused by you
You claimed to be protecting me
But in reality, you frightened me
Your dastardly lies of abuse
Confused us all
No harm ever came to you nor me
Your anger always boiled in you
But no one understood why
You bore threats and promises of retribution
No one knew just how or when you'd strike
We all lived in fear and dread
Your leaving home was the best day
If only your threats and reign of terror
You had kept to yourself forever after

Leeza Wilson

Alzheimer's

You are a wicked illness
You are a thief
Who steals minds and memories
You creep up on some
While others you attack at once
You break our hearts
As our loved ones forget
Who we are and the life we've shared
You pull them back to childhood
Then in the end your cruelness mounts
You take our loved ones away for good

How Do You See Me?

I wonder…
How do you see me?
Am I even somewhat useful,
Or just someone you tolerate?
I strive to give my all
I do the best I can
I want to be accepted
But can't shake that nagging feeling
That no one cares if I'm here or not
I wonder if anyone would miss me
If I left and never returned
Would my departure be filled
With everyone's rejoicing?
Would anyone remember me,
Or instantly set my memory free?
I would miss you all
And forever hold your memory dear
But how do you see me?

Cry

The tears come easily
Far too much so
My heart breaks
A little more each day
For my sins
I will forever pay
I bury my head in shame
And cry the pain away
There's nothing more to do
For my actions
The consequences I must suffer
The scars to my heart and soul,
Will mark who I am from now on
To cry is the only way to cleanse my soul.

Dreams

The dreams have started again
They haunt me all night long
Changing form and magnitude
They go from strange to foreboding
How I wish they'd go away
And let me sleep in peace
Even in the day
There is no reprieve
They stay in my brain
Trying to come to terms
With whatever they could mean

Torn

The early years were hard
Trying to have a happy, normal childhood
It didn't prove an easy feat
I was torn you see
Between love and fear and innocence
I wanted to love you, dear sister
But your mania frightened me
You told me, "I love you."
You said you were protecting me
"From what?" I always asked
I couldn't believe the lies you told
I never experienced your reality
How could you love someone
That you treated so mean?
With me you never wanted to play
You always told me to go away
I only wanted to spend time with you
But I'd stay away to make you happy
Even though it made me feel lonely
And an unwanted nuisance
And what pain you caused our parents!
Worst yet, you didn't even care

It was like the pain of others
Brought you the greatest joy
But I survived ok
My make-believe friends
Never let me down
Or caused me to feel torn
I made my own reality
And wished I had been the only born.

Leeza Wilson

Where's the Music

Where's the music that once played?
It was the light of my life
It was the ray that brightened my days
But silent it has gone
I just need one tune
To clear the fog surrounding me
Oh the power of just one song!
It lifts my spirits to the heavens
The best song is of old
An 80's tune that takes me back
It lifts the weight of the world
That pulls me under
Freeing my soul to soar
Where's the music that lifts the weight?
I need the music
To just play, play, play
Endlessly throughout my days

Poverty

Have you ever felt the painful burn of poverty?
Have you felt the fear of never knowing
If there will be money for food
Or enough to pay rent and electric?
Have you felt the frustration of
Working all the time and still can't provide?
Have you felt the shame of poverty?
Have you felt the desperation of trying
Your best to keep the lights on
And fearing for the little one in your care?
How will you cook for him with no power, and
How will you bathe him with no running water?
The system we live in is corrupt
It's run by the wealthy and greedy
Who have never felt the pain of poverty
They do not understand the pain
And mental anguish that consumes
The struggling soul

Leeza Wilson

My Mistake

I trusted you with my soul
I poured my heart out to you
But clearly you were not ready
For now you will barely talk to me
I see it clearly now
That my trust in you was a mistake
Now I feel ashamed and embarrassed
I wish I could take it all back
Never more will I burden you
Locked tight I will keep my heart
And silent I will stay forever more
Never again will I make the same mistake

Haiku Poems

Moonlit Bay

At night on the bay
The moonlight so calmly lays
So serene I say

Butterflies

Butterflies, oh my!
So beautiful in the skies
As on winds drift by

Leeza Wilson

Flowers

Tulips and daisies
In meadows so beautiful
Dancing in the sun

The River's Bend

At the river's bend
Where the mountains touch the sky
My paradise lies

The Mausoleum

Red mausoleum
Body of Lenin within
Chill of death around

The Eiffel Tower

The Eiffel tower
Warming the fall night in lights
Moon remains behind

Black Cat

Cat black as night
Fall leaves rustling under feet
Moon rising on high

Autumn

Full moon in the sky
Fog forming over the ground
Pumpkins on porches

Rose

A rose so gorgeous
To you no comparison
Our love never fades

Masterpiece

Like a masterpiece
Across the land meadows bloom
Painted by God's hand

Birds

Birds in the bushes
Taking flight into the sky
Freedom in glory

Things That Wow

Wonders of the world
Acrobats in performance
Things that wow the mind

Other Books By Leeza Wilson

Children's Books

My Grandpa is Extra Sweet: Diabetic Emergencies

The Germ Squad: Colds, Flu, and Stomach Bugs

Poetry Books

A Bouquet of Poems

My Secret Garden and Other Poems for Children

Follow Leeza on Social Media

www.facebook.com/leezatheauthor
www.twitter.com/leezatheauthor
www.instagram.com/leezatheauthor
www.pinterest.com/leezatheauthor

About the Author

Leeza grew up with a fascination for notebooks and writing utensils. She began reading and writing at age four, mostly self-taught due to her independent and determined personality. She has had a love of books and reading her entire life. And from her love of reading has grown a love for writing. She writes in the genres of romance, mystery, suspense, historical, literary fiction, poetry, and children's. She is currently writing a children's series, more poems, and a romantic suspense spy series.

When not writing, she enjoys drawing and painting; spending time with her family; listening to music; volunteering with her local fire department; and playing the piano and guitar. She lives with her son, two cats, and Chihuahua in the Smoky Mountains of Tennessee.

Please Write a Review

Thank you for reading my book. It is my deepest wish that you had a pleasant reading experience and found the poems enjoyable. Whether you did or didn't, please feel free to get in touch and let me know what you thought. I love hearing from my readers and I always try my best to respond to emails and social media messages from my fans.

As any author will tell you, reviews are so very important in helping our books get noticed. Reviews help authors reach more readers by letting them know if a book is worth reading or not. So I rely a lot on reviews to help readers find my books and know if they're worthy of investing their time in to read. It only takes a couple of minutes to write a brief review of what you thought of the book. So if you can take a minute to write an honest review, I would greatly appreciate it, even if it's a negative review. All reviews matter, whether they're 1 star or 5 stars, a small essay or just one word. I value your honest feedback.

Thank YOU

Leeza Wilson

www.ingramcontent.com/pod-product-compliance
Lightning Source LLC
Chambersburg PA
CBHW052104110526
44591CB00013B/2352